BEFORE I HAD A MOTHER

A Calumet Childhood in Pieces

TERRY CAESAR

Copyright © 2010 by Terry Caesar. All rights reserved.

Except for use in any review, no part of this book may be reproduced in whole or in part, or stored in a retrieval system or transmitted in any form or by any means without written permission of the author.

ISBN: 978-1-935591-00-9

First printing, February 2010

This edition was printed by Grelin Press
P.O. Box 367, New Kensington, PA 15068
Tel: (724) 334-8240 grelinpress@aol.com

To Eva, who brought me back

Table of Contents

Introduction 7

Part I 13
Galoshes 15
Altar Boy 19

Part II 23
Gramps 25
Ziggy 28
Ronnie 31
Aunt Eleanor 34
Pepper 37

Part III
Culture 41

Before Televison 43
Comics 47
Guns 51
Movies 55

Society 59

Sports 61
Gender 65
Food 69
Sex 73

Part IV 77

George Gip 79
Mary 83
Flying Away 87
Hal 91

Part V 95

Mother 97

About the Author 101

Introduction

This book is a memoir of the first ten years of my life, with my grandparents in Calumet, Michigan. How did I come to live with them? Why only ten years? What does the title mean? Although the answers gradually emerge, I've tried to keep these questions at bay, in the hope that my personal story will be able to express something more resonant of what it was like to grow up in Calumet in the mid-40s and early 50s.

Most people in the United States are still, I think, only vaguely aware of the Upper Peninsula, and entirely unaware of Calumet, which lies at the far tip, curving out like a fin into Lake Superior. Calumet remains almost too remote to be exotic. Yet if, as the British novelist wrote, "the past is a far country," Calumet is an excellent place to have had a past. I was lucky enough to have it be mine.

Of course to some extent its themes are perennial ones–discoveries of life's elemental facts, dreams of faraway places . . . but wait: if I did have these discoveries, I didn't have these dreams. During the first ten years of my life, Calumet was wonderfully—wondrously—sufficient to me, and so I've tried to write of it in a way that expresses its self-sufficiency, through a series of short chapters grouped around various people or subjects.

These chapters finally have the character more of essays than stories. My childhood might have unfolded with unremarkable immediacy and daily continuity. But I don't experience it this way in the present, and what I remember now provides the only basis for representing anything. There's no concealing the present, especially not when contemplating the past. Therefore, many of these chapters indulge in speculation about what might have once been lived, if only because it can't quite be remembered.

Put another way: I had a childhood. I don't have a theory of childhood–at most, only a conviction about how to write about it. In most respects, my account could not be more different than Penelope Lively's memoir, *Oleander, Jacaranda*. We agree, though, that the child's "way of seeing" is indeed almost lost in adult life. "You can stare," she continues, "you can observe–but within the head there is now the unstoppable obscuring onward rush of things. It is no longer possible simply to see, without the accompanying internal din of meditation."

Such a "din" is everywhere in the following pages. Other than the fact that, for me at least, there would otherwise be nothing—no pages—without it, I plead another reason: I was somebody always absorbed in that din, even as a kid. You can see it in the precious few pictures (a few reprinted here) I have somehow retained of my Calumet years. I look abstracted and serious. Some kids are like that. I was one. I don't even think it had anything to do with not—or rather not yet—having a mother.

The last time I revisited Calumet was September 13, 2001. Two days earlier, my wife and I were about to make our way to Detroit International, for a flight to Osaka, when the motel television screen flashed pictures of the first of the Twin Towers ablaze. The airport was closed an hour later. My cousin—my only living relative—had already driven away to Calumet in our car We didn't need it in Japan. Now what? Just remain at the motel? Our flight couldn't be rescheduled until nearly another week.

Next day we decided to rent a car and drive to Calumet, stopping somewhere off U.S. 75 overnight, a hundred miles before making it to Mackinaw City, as planned. But this present wasn't a time for plans. In fact, suddenly it seemed like time had ceased to exist. So we headed for Calumet, disoriented, not so much as if we were fleeing from history but as if we were trying to regain time. But what time? Once more, the past?

Too bad it isn't possible to go straight to some pure temporal essence, bypassing place entirely. As it is, or was, late the following day: poor Calumet, again--its old brick buildings so shabby, its wide streets so aimless, its newer shops so hopeful. Calumet is not Proustian. It's still poor—in population, natural resources, geographical location, just as I remember it from when I grew up there. But there is one immense difference: fifty years ago Calumet comprised all I had in the world and Calumet was all I needed of the world.

Over the course of the subsequent few post-9/11 days Eva and I visited with my cousin, drove around, saw both a Calumet High Friday night football game and a Saturday afternoon Michigan Tech game, and lit candles at the grave of both my grandparents. Gramps and Granny lived at 310 Seventh Street. The owner of one of Calumet's largest gift shops bought the house from Gramps in 1976. During our visit seven years previous, the owner was kind enough to take us through. The house was so different from my memory that I may as well never have lived in it.

The porch was now too narrow, the living room too small. The dining room was the center of the family's living space, whereas I was shocked to realize that to me as a child it had meant little; we ate in the kitchen. Where was Granny's pantry? Gone. What was the color of the wallpaper when I lived here? Another unrecoverable memory. Virtually the only thing in the house that I could make emotional contact with was Granny's old stone washbasin downstairs.

I used to sit there while she pressed clothes through the ringer of the white enamel washer next to the washbasin. Now late in 2001 the day before we left Calumet in order to return to Detroit, I suddenly developed a powerful urge to see this washbasin again. But of course it wasn't the washbasin I wanted to see. It was Granny and some image of myself, age six or eight or ten, each of us as well as the ritual of washing enclosed by the whole house as if sealed off from time.

How to refuse the tug of this image? And yet it must be refused or else you'll cease to live in the present. The brief, improbable post-9/11 days of my wife and me in Calumet were at an end. Time to become immersed back into history once more. We had jobs in Japan. Time to reenter, well, time—in which, for example, my life in 310 Seventh Street was relegated to the past, once more. I didn't need to return to Calumet in order to be aware of this. But it helped. Whether in memory or in person, Calumet always helps.

Writing an autobiography is as much an act of consigning to the past what of it is irretrievable as it is of recovering what of it has endured. A week before I began to write the first of these pages, an autobiography about Calumet—of all things!—would have seemed the farthest thing from my mind. Now I wonder why the past can't just *stay put*, where, as we say, it belongs? Must it first be, precisely, "put"—picked up and then put down— as you would handle any object, a special one that had to be retrieved first.

Calumet set in post-9/11 is not part of this book. I've kept its conscious focus exclusively on the Calumet of my childhood. Yet more recently the intersection of a sudden narrative of global proportions and an abiding experience of purely personal scale is strange enough to give me pause. One of the things the intersection suggests is that you can never predict how stories will relate to each other, or how variously and deviously some stories can only proceed on the basis of recreating an apparently innocent past.

Indeed, before some fact of overwhelming power, such a characterization of what came before appears almost inescapable. However, I hope I've avoided it here, despite—no, because of my title. I wasn't so much innocent when I grew up in Calumet as ignorant. Worse, I wasn't sure about the sources of my ignorance. I'm more certain now, and so I've tried to name them. I can't really speak about post-9/11 United States. I can speak about my own experience.

Undoubtedly much in it before I had a mother is either lost or incalculable. Not even the powerful perceptions of Lively, for example, can purport to see her experience whole, rather than in pieces. Yet not all is lost, and not all in the same way. It seems to me that if the past cannot be restored, it can be reclaimed—consciously, purposefully, faithfully, bit by bit. All you have to do is know where to look. Fortunately for me, it is in Calumet.

I.

Granny and Me

Galoshes

I wore thick, elaborately laced rubber boots, called "rubbers" or "galoshes," anytime I left the house in winter. My waist-length jacket had a hood lined with fur. I looked like an Eskimo. Winters in the Upper Peninsula are long, cold, and piled high with snow—over 250 inches, annually.

I loved winters: the crunch of the snow under your feet when the snow was hard, the downy softness when it was fresh. There's a way you can plow through heavy snow, pushing it along with your legs as you trudge so that it feels like you're establishing some right to walk with each new step.

In snow, Calumet was transformed into a pure white version of itself. No more boarded-up houses or dingy buildings, testimony to a little town fallen on hard times since decades before, when the copper mines closed. The whole world became a child's version when it snowed. There were only a few differences to see, and you didn't have to pay much attention to them because finally the only distinction to make was, more snow or less.

Calumet was—and remains—a very small town. Only eight hundred people or so. Railroad tracks stretching past a railroad station divided the houses. You could walk anywhere, and I did. Snow promised a sort of universal ease of access. You just put on your galoshes, opened the door, and plowed out, easily or slowly, depending on the snowfall.

Sometimes, it was fun just to keep plowing, going nowhere. My grandparents' house was only two blocks from Fifth Street, the center of town, where there were a couple of restaurants, a department store, and a drug store. The other stores meant little to me. Most of the time, I just wanted to be *out*. The world was totally exterior. Snow just confirmed it.

Did my relation to snow change from, say, the time I was four to the time I was eight? Sure. For one thing, by eight I was going to school and had discovered snow banks. My classmates and I used to get out of school—Morrison was just half a block away across the street for me—and play "King of the Hill." The game was simple: you climbed a big snow bank, dodging snowballs and pushing other kids, until you got to the top.

Your reign didn't last long. Soon other kids deposed you, and you had to start all over again, sometimes from the bottom, where the snow was in hard chunks, like stones. But I don't remember anybody getting hurt playing "King of the Hill." It was just a dumb game that enabled us to thrash around in the snow as if it was a body of water and we were learning how to swim.

There was skiing, on a hill perhaps a mile from where I lived. A moving cable stretched from top to bottom. We grabbed onto the cable and skied down. Why was I never any good at this? I don't even remember having any skis. Were we too poor? Was it as if there was so much snow it seemed idle to learn to glide across its surface, when the real fun was to dive into it, as if we were fish?

Calumet had a professional hockey team, the Calumet Radars. By the time I was eight I was going to night games at the armory—it wasn't very far—with other kids. I never learned to skate. We just vied for the honor of cleaning the ice between periods, plowing the rink with outsized snow shovels alongside two or three other kids, each wearing galoshes. Only a few of my friends had skates. No skates when we played hockey among ourselves, which was always in the street, whacking pieces of ice with cheap wooden hockey sticks. They often cracked.

By the time I started going to the Radars games, my grandmother must have been worried about me. I remember once coming home groaning, very sick to my stomach. I couldn't understand why. She could. I had gotten so excited being out I stuffed myself with hot dogs, popcorn, and ice cream. So Granny chastised me. I had to promise, never again. She had to believe me.

One winter day I remember vividly. I wasn't as young as two; I wasn't as old as ten. The day was, or is now, out of time. I had stayed outside too long. Playing "King of the Hill?" Playing hockey? I don't remember. It scarcely matters. Kids often stay out too long. That's why they're kids—even the ones who are old enough to know better, and then to act heedless of what they know. This day, I was a kid like that.

When I got home Granny was worried and I had begun shivering. She helped me out of my galoshes. She hugged me. She went to the kitchen to get me something hot to drink. What I remember most vividly, though, is how everything felt so warm, so comfortable, so *inside*. No matter how much you love winter, it's always cold and sometimes it's dangerously cold. No matter how much you love winter, it's better to come home to somebody who loves you.

Altar Boy

Both my grandmother, Josephine Jankoviak, and my grandfather, John Tobola, were Polish. Therefore, they were Catholic. Therefore, I was raised a Catholic. And therefore, in due time, I became an altar boy.

Weddings were the best. You got tips. Once a groom gave the other altar boy and me each a ten-dollar bill. It took all the sober altar-boyness we could muster (I never quite figured out the role) not to exclaim, "ten bucks," fall to our knees, and give thanks to God.

Most common were the early-morning Masses. St. Joseph's Church was only a block away from home, behind the school on the corner. I wish I could remember zealously donning my winter clothes and dutifully plowing through dim winter light until I got inside to the sacristy. I can't. I can barely visualize the red sandstone church itself with its two spires.

Was the cassock—a full-length robe—altar boys wore always red? In my imagination now, it was so. Similarly, was the surplice—an embroidered, large-sleeved gown fitted over the cassock to knee length—always white? Surely it was. The cassock seemed merely official, like a uniform. The surplice felt flouncy, girlish. But we never would have uttered the judgment, "girlish," then.

I was an altar boy in the 40s. From the perspective of today, this might appear a golden decade. Children memorized the Apostles Creed unquestioningly, nobody dreamed of anything sexual to do with priests, everybody took Communion, and all the Masses were in Latin. Certainly it would no more have occurred to me to question the rule of the Catholic Church than to question the existence of winter.

Yet it seems to me now I was barely more devout than a pagan. Take Latin. I memorized all the altar boy's responses during the Mass. But what I remember is holding some part of myself away from the words rather than sinking wholly into them. Another boy and I used to look at each other and snigger at a priest who often dribbled the consecrated wine from his mouth. I always muttered impatiently to myself at another priest who said the Mass too slowly.

The altar boy moment I liked best was at Communion, when I got to put the shiny metal plate under the chin of each recipient of the sacred Host, lest it be defiled by falling to the floor. My role felt as crucial to the ceremony as Father's—we always referred to priests as "Father"—when he placed the Host on each individual's tongue.

But too many of those tongues seemed comic to me—darting in and out of the mouth like a little animal atop a squeeze toy. More inward sniggering. One old woman (most of those who attended early morning Mass were old women) was instant drama each time she took Communion. Miraculously, the Host never slid from her tongue onto my plate. Each time I wished that it would. Sometimes, I even wondered what would happen if it hit the floor.

Did the moment of actually taking Communion seem too intimate to me where Granny was concerned, and so I have no distinct memory of her, as opposed to every other recipient? Or at this moment was her mouth just another mouth, her tongue just as unsteady or lively? Perhaps, before her, I was a bit too self-conscious about being an altar boy, if not about being insufficiently devout.

The real scandal was Gramps. Granny attended Mass regularly, and I accompanied her on Sunday. Each Sunday morning we waited for Gramps to get dressed in his blue suit. Each Sunday we hoped he would join us to walk to Church. Each Sunday he pleaded that he would rather go "out" instead. Just "out." Granny never asked where. Either she knew or it didn't matter. I didn't know and it did matter, but it would have mattered more if Granny had shouted at Gramps. In my memory, she never did. The two of us, long-suffering according to our different lights, just trudged to church together. Secretly, I was happier this way. Maybe she was too.

Granny died of a heart attack after three days in the hospital. There was a new John Wayne film at the movie theater and I wanted to go after she was hospitalized. Gramps didn't let me. When Granny died everybody thought it was wonderful that I could be the altar boy at her funeral. I didn't agree. But nobody asked me. So what felt like a final time I went through the motions. They didn't give my grief form and expression.

Granny's death was too sudden. It wasn't like winter or the Catholic Church. I couldn't accept it. The day before the funeral, there was a "viewing" at the local funeral home. From a distance I could see Granny in the open coffin. She looked just like Granny always looked. How could she be dead? What did it mean to be "dead?"

Probably sensing my fear and incomprehension, my Uncle Carl (Gramps and Granny had two sons) seized my arm and marched me to the coffin. Then he grabbed my neck, pushed my face down, and forced my lips against Granny's. They were cold. They didn't move. How could this be Granny? The best thing about being an altar boy is that although you get to be included in the great ceremonies of life and death, you aren't expected to get too close.

II.

Aunt Eleanor and Me

Gramps

Gramps was what is known as a "rockhound." He collected rocks. His collection was one of the largest in the country. Ceiling-high wooden shelves stretching all over the basement were piled high with boxes of malachite and quartz and God knows what else. I never learned.

Once in awhile Gramps would take a "sample" of crystal and twist it around in his hand. "See, Terry, look at the hollow here and how the light reflects." No use. I just stared, trying to be interested and failing every time. He may as well have been talking to, well, a stone.

What I really liked to do is to walk with Gramps when he went on his "rock-hunting expeditions." The same geological distinctiveness whereby Calumet became the center of the Copper Country (until the copper was mined out by the 20s) made the area rich in stones of all sorts. Gramps peered intently at the ground, while I was content to tag along.

He walked too fast. I was always asking Gramps to slow down. He would. We must have talked of daily, inconsequential things—the weather, what Granny would cook for dinner. I don't remember a single one. Perhaps this means that I didn't put any emotional pressure on Gramps, as I probably would have had he been my father rather than my grandfather.

Gramps was a clerk at the post office. I hardly ever had occasion to go there. Whenever I did, my grandfather looked odd at a tiny window, usually with the brim of an accountant's cap across his forehead. The person I knew was Gramps, a gruff, silent man with a stiff, lean body and an amazingly tender way of uttering my name, "Terry." I loved the way he said my name.

How did he address my grandmother? Did the two of them ever touch? When did they meet? Where? Were their parents born in America? None of the questions that interest me now would have been ones I either noticed or asked then. What mattered then was that Gramps and Granny kept their distance from each other, but not so much distance that I had to agonize about why.

Gramps picked his nose at the table. Granny hated this. He was cheap. She joked to me about it. He always promised to take us on rides in his new Pontiac. (Gramps traded in the old one every year.) Granny and I conspired to get him at least to take us to Copper Harbor, where we could see Lake Superior and walk along the stony beach.

I always sat in the middle in the front seat. When I got a little older, Gramps let me sit in his lap and hold the steering wheel, which Granny didn't think was a good idea. I'll bet it was his idea, not hers, to get me a bicycle for Christmas. I promptly named it, "Trigger," after the horse of my favorite cowboy, Roy Rodgers.

What do grandfathers do? Tell their grandsons stories? I don't remember any Gramps told me. Mainly, he was just there, at the fringes of my experience, a figure of authority but not definition. For the most part, Gramps left me to Granny, and Granny was happy to have me. Gramps retired somewhere else, usually downstairs with his rocks.

He also had a garage out back where he puttered. In winter, two thick planks of wood ran above the snow from the back door of the house to the front door of the garage. Once, Gramps killed a duck and hung it upside down on that door. I slumped down before the limp body when I saw it and cried. How could Gramps do such a thing?

I never learned if he did. But I believe I know why I have such a vivid memory of this dead duck. It seems like the action of a father, not a grandfather. Fathers kill things. They strike fear into the hearts of their sons with their power. On the other hand, grandfathers nurture things. The source of their authority is different—quieter, steadier, based less on conflict and more on shared, even unspoken, agreement. The man whom I hugged goodnight, despite his bristly beard (I can still feel how it scratched me) was my grandfather not my father. Gramps could never kill a duck.

There was only one place to which we went that didn't make sense: Sego's. Sego's was a tiny grocery way down on the shabbiest end of Main Street. There was a rickety wooden front door with a bell that tinkled when you opened it. The plastered walls were peeling. Some tables and chairs were back to one side, and usually a few men sat at them. Gramps would plunk me down at one of these tables, order me a soda, chat with his buddies, and eventually step into some rear area through a doorway covered by a cheap cloth curtain.

Why did he take me here? What did he do when he went back there? I wasn't really pained when I sat at Sego's. Just puzzled, pleasantly. As usual, Gramps managed to include me in his sort of dry, gentle way in the world. His lank body and shock of jet-black hair must have cut a handsome figure. He asked me never to tell Granny that we had gone to Sego's and I never did.

Ziggy

I had two friends: Ronnie and Ziggy. Ronnie's father owned a—or rather, the—meat-packing plant. He was rich, at least in Calumet's terms. Ziggy didn't have a father. He was poor, in anybody's terms. His house was more like a shack, a wooden contraption down one side of a hill in the midst of a clump of trees.

Why was Ziggy my friend? Perhaps because of his carefree good nature. Moon-faced Ziggy liked to screw around, do stupid things. More self-conscious or smart kids like me respond to their opposites and this response, I suppose, then becomes its own reason.

One thing Ziggy and I liked to do is smoke cigarettes. When did I start smoking? I don't remember, except Ziggy and I were among a group of kids who smoked. "Peer pressure?" I doubt it. There were some kids who smoked. I was among them. I smoked, too.

Of course we couldn't do so in public. It's not so much that we feared punishment. It's that we cherished secrecy. So three or four or five or six of us met in back alleys. It was delicious to light up. Nobody knew but us. That we smoked became the stuff of what we knew and that they—adults—didn't.

How did we get the cigarettes? We stole them. I don't remember stealing any myself. (My thing was candy and comic books.) The other kids did—sometimes cartons, which was always a great day. Ziggy hid the cigarettes.

One of our favorite places to smoke (always after school) was down among the rotted beams and crumbled stones of an abandoned building on Fifth Street. Such a dumpy site must have suited our desire to appear (to ourselves) dangerous and dissolute.

We didn't constitute a "gang." A gang defines itself over against other gangs. But in Calumet at this time among preteen (not to say prepubescent) kids there were no other gangs. Just groups of kids who did dumb things and needed to discover they were dumb.

Our respective parents would have greatly hastened the discovery, which was why we spent considerable time, while we puffed and inhaled, devising schemes to prevent them from finding out. One was drinking lime juice.

I don't know who dreamed up this remedy for removing the smell of cigarettes from your breath. We all believed it. None more than me, and I especially favored the Fifth Street site because it's just down from the drug store, at whose counter I could order a lime before going home, a mere two blocks away.

One smoke-besotted afternoon I duly sat down and ordered. I was alone, as usual. We were all just kids. Time to get home for supper. Our cherished collectivity had to break up. Nobody had any ambition to extend it in order to threaten the social order, which consisted, in part, of people who could buy cigarettes and smoke whole packs of them to their heart's content.

I had some forboding this day. Granny knew I was smoking. I was sure she knew. Or else I was so afraid she knew that the fear counted for certainty. All the lime juice in the drug store, no, in the whole Upper Peninsula, would not be able to conceal the truth.

Ziggy never seemed to be afraid of his mother finding out. Ziggy never seemed to be afraid of anything. That's why I liked Ziggy, that's why we all liked Ziggy.

Perhaps that's also why the parents of the other kids didn't like Ziggy. At least this was one thing I didn't have to worry about: Granny had never met him.

Finally I couldn't delay going home any longer. I wasn't afraid that Granny would hit me. This was inconceivable. I was afraid that I would disappoint her. If this wasn't inconceivable to her (I was terribly, terribly spoiled) it was close. A seven or eight year-old grandson who *smoked cigarettes*? That was the sort of thing a Ziggy would do, not her Terry.

I walked in the front door. Granny appeared so I could hug her. She was a heavy woman. Her body felt at once soft and firm. As I put my arms around her waist, I tried to keep my mouth to one side. Maybe, I hoped, if she smelled smoke, she would get it confused with Gramps. Gramps smoked cigars.

Granny didn't seem to smell a thing.

Was it possible? Not a thing. From the perspective of the present, it's possible to believe that in fact Granny did know—at this time, at all other times; she simply indulged me in one more thing. But in the past that I lived well over fifty years ago, Granny said not a word. And I can still recall my own emotion. I wasn't relieved. I was disappointed.

Not in Granny, and not in myself. I was disappointed that life turns out to be not so simple as being found out or not being found out doing something wrong. How can it be instead that sometimes you want to be somebody else? I was Terry, my grandmother's own. Yet this particular day anyway it was as if I wanted to be Ziggy. For all I knew, Ziggy didn't even have a mother.

Ronnie

I remember less about Ronnie than Ziggy. He was taller, older, *meaner* than Ziggy. I'm pretty sure of that. Perhaps he was a grade ahead of me. I certainly visited his house at least once, whose flat rectangular sprawl was very different than the erect, two-story wooden clapboards of the rest of Calumet, including ours. Is this ranch-style house the basis for my sense was Ronnie was rich?

Another thing about Ronnie: he was tall and blonde. Girls liked him. It seems improbable now that this fact could this have mattered to me when I was eight or nine years old. Yet I believe it did. It's as if being near the heat of Ronnie's more emphatic sexuality drew attention away from my own nascent, cooler energies. I could feel safe, and safely develop.

One incident having to do with Ronnie stands out so vividly that it effectively obscures all others. I can't explain how it illuminates my friendship with Ronnie. It does demonstrate, though, how my friendship with Ronnie provided one basis for my relationship to life.

I can almost locate on a map of memory where the "slaughterhouse" (that's what everybody termed it) of Ronnie's father was. It was somewhere down on Fifth Street—my street—in an area where things were made rather than sold. Kids didn't have much reason to go there.

So why one day did Ronnie take me there? I don't know. It's tempting to speculate now that he took me there because I was afraid to go. And of course it's even more tempting to say that I went because I wanted to demonstrate to Ronnie that I wasn't afraid. But I was. Ronnie knew it.

One often hears that kids who grow up in small towns have a closer, more raw relation to life. Often what this means is merely that they see animals that people eat get killed first. Not me. As far as I can recall, I had only the bloody carcass of my grandfather's dead duck to bring to this particular day at the slaughterhouse.

I hated it as soon as we walked in. Men strode around with blood-soaked leather aprons. The walls were stained black; who knew with what? Worst of all was the rancid, briny stench lifting off stacks of animals hides arranged all across a floor half the size of a football field. I wanted to throw up.

Did Ronnie hope I would? If so, probably not consciously. Then he wouldn't have been my friend. Yet surely he wanted to stretch, or test, the bonds of friendship, especially at an age when these bonds are so subject to chance or accident; the heart of the reason why I don't remember much about Ronnie is that I don't understand how I could have been friends with him.

Onward we went, past the disgusting stacks, to the back of the slaughterhouse. I heard snorting noises and strange thumps. It was scary. Ronnie must have known it. But he wasn't scared and so I couldn't be. It never occurred to me that he couldn't be scared because I was. Perhaps Ronnie held out the prospect of meeting his father. No father ever materialized.

We stood beside a square concrete pen. The floor was slimy. In the middle of the pen there was a cow held still by ropes stretched through his nostrils and around his feet. Did Ronnie tell me what was going to happen? I must have suddenly felt more terrified than the cow, which looked crazed.

We saw a man with a sledgehammer. He lifted it and plunged it down hard on the head of the cow. It grunted. Its legs splayed. The man lifted the sledgehammer and hit the cow on the head again. Its legs must have splayed more. Maybe the man hit the cow a third or even a fourth time. There must have been a lot of blood. I only remember the sight of the cow collapsed to one side, faintly heaving with remaining life. How could it not be dead?

We didn't linger. In fact, I don't remember anything more of what happened this day, once the cow was driven to the floor of that pen. Did Ronnie look at my terror—surely I failed to conceal it—with satisfaction? Or at that moment did he regret having taken me to his father's slaughterhouse, whatever the pretext?

Some memories are so vivid they become hallucinatory. Few have resonated over the whole course of my life than this one of the slaughtered cow. It really happened, just the way I've described it. What I can't describe is why it has continued so vivid. At least some of the reason must be because the experience is not only about a traumatically slaughtered cow.

It's also about Ronnie—about how this experience shattered our friendship. It must have. But this day happened too long ago. I can't recover any more of it than how the slaughter at the center still pulses with just enough faint light to suggest the presence of a more encompassing darkness. Ronnie led me right up to the glare of more experience than I could handle. Then I switched off the light.

Aunt Eleanor

Uncle Carl lived in Calumet. He had a wife I didn't like, probably because she was emotionally cluttered with two other kids of her own, each one younger than me. Gramps and Granny's other son, my Uncle John, lived in Georgia. Once he visited. I remember a fat, jovial man—a Santa without a beard—who brought me a lot of presents.

It's easy to say now that I loved Uncle John as much as I hated Uncle Carl. Too easy. Uncle John was easy to love because he lived far away and all I had to do was write him after receiving his letters. Uncle Carl was tougher. He had a temper and showed it each time he visited our house. Yet I remember the times he took me along on his mail route, and I loved feeling the wind of the open door or trying quickly to stuff letters into mail boxes.

Besides my mother, to whom I wrote (she lived in California), and my father, to whom I didn't write (I didn't know where he lived), I had no other relatives than these two uncles. But there was another woman who visited often: Aunt Eleanor. My grandparents liked her. She was fun—a bustle of fur coats, odd hats, darting smiles and silly jokes.

Aunt Eleanor had a husband, Rudy, who always accompanied her. Rudy ran a car dealership. Sometimes I either called him or was bid to call him, "Uncle Rudy." But he wasn't actually my uncle, which is probably why in my mind's eye he is always in the background, while his wife, who apparently really was my aunt, provides all the animation of each visit.

Yet if Eleanor was my aunt, she only suggested a larger mystery: my father's side of the family. Not only did I have no contact with my father. I had no knowledge of his family, with the singular exception of Aunt Eleanor, who must have been his sister. Even so, why her and her alone from this side in my experience?

It's easy to imagine a story. Eleanor was damned if she was going to let my mother, her brothers, and her parents effectively seal me away from my father's side of the family. So one fine day she just stepped up to the door of Gramps and Granny, demanded to be let in, and entered, whereupon she almost burst into tears at the sight of her little nephew. Rudy carried presents.

Why did my grandparents open the door? Calumet was such a small town. Perhaps they had some separate relation with Eleanor. Or perhaps Gramps bought each year's new Pontiac from Rudy. It's also possible that Granny or Gramps felt guilty at having to maintain the complete absence of paternity in my life. Although the sister of my father, she appeared as it were under the sign of maternity.

Aunt Eleanor had no children. This is the most obvious explanation not only why she alone was permitted access to me but why she wanted—or in my fiction, demanded—it. And what she brought was a specifically maternal feeling, different than the soft, expansive love of my grandmother. Aunt Eleanor's love—I don't know what else to call it—was sharper, more acute.

I felt it literally on her fingertips. She had wondrously long fingernails. My grandmother had hands, not fingers, much less fingertips. Aunt Eleanor used to scratch my back; I couldn't wait to lift up my shirt. Granny, by contrast, caressed me. She could afford to take my body for granted.

Did Eleanor and Rudy visit me from the very beginning of the time I arrived in Calumet right up until the time I left Calumet in 1952? I don't know. Now there's no way to find out. In my memory Aunt Eleanor always becomes a species of Fairy Godmother, a beneficent substitute for the real mother, who is inexplicably absent. She may be dead, she may be angry. In any case, the Fairy Godmother comes forward with gifts but most of all with the gift of her own presence.

I do have the vaguest knowledge that one day Rudy had a heart attack and died. If so, perhaps Eleanor moved away from Calumet—a lovely woman still (I remember she had a angular bright face) and now a widow in an area so rife with old Eastern European traditions that she may as well have been required to wear widow's weeds. There may have even been a moment when she came to say good-bye to me.

At the end of this moment I surely asked her to scratch my back for the last time. I was only seven, or eight, or ten years old. Hearing my request, Gramps poked a finger in his nose. Granny suppressed a tear. Aunt Eleanor did what she always did, and does to this day. She takes off her gloves—she always wore gloves—and helps me pull my shirt up. When she reaches for my skin I am already beginning to shiver with delight.

Pepper

I ought to have loved Pepper more. I've loved dogs all my life. Pepper was my first dog. Only he wasn't mine, and during the years I lived with him I must have sensed in some unknown childhood way a stranger connection with Pepper that I couldn't understand and that troubled me.

One morning he was dead at the foot of the basement stairs. My grandmother found him and screamed. My grandfather went down and brought the body upstairs. That night, he and I buried Pepper in a forest outside town.

Say I was ten years old. Perhaps Pepper was the same age. It seemed he had always lived with us. He was a Scottie, an uncommon, almost precious breed for the Upper Peninsula at that time. Everyone would exclaim how "cute" Pepper was, meaning "unusual" or "tiny."

I didn't think Pepper was so cute. Once he bit me when I was very young. I used to show people the teeth marks on my wrist, as if to say, "if you think he's so cute, how can you explain this?" Everyone thought the teeth marks were cute.

Because he was so small and stubby-legged, Pepper never went anywhere with Gramps and me on our walks. I don't think I ever showed him to Ziggy or Ronnie. On the other hand, he seems like the sort of dog Aunt Eleanor would have liked, and surely when she visited he was eager to roll over so she could scratch his tummy.

I don't have many pictures of my life in Calumet. There's only one of Pepper, which is really a picture of me, a chubby, fair-haired boy, facing the camera with his downcast eyes. My left arm is upraised. I look oddly stricken. Pepper is seated just behind me, tipping away to the right.

This ought to be a picture of "A Boy and His Dog." It's not. Some sort of canvass bag, like a book bag or a tote bag, is slung over my shoulder. If anything is dictating my emotion, whatever it is, it's this bag, not Pepper, who appears as if he just happens to be in the picture, a typical furry Scottie, mouth open, bright-eyed.

More likely, though, the picture just "captures" a moment in time, in terms of some circumstance that is not visible in the picture. The dog, even the bag, are incidental to the reason the picture was taken. In fact, that reason itself is not visible now, if it ever was on a day sixty years ago.

A few years ago my mother chanced to remark to my wife than in fact Pepper was her dog. I was shocked. Had I not known this before? How *could* I not have known this before? Surely there was no reason for Gramps or Granny to conceal Pepper's origins from me. Now it seems to me as if these origins explain the heart of my attitude toward the dog.

If my mother brought Pepper to her parents before me, why? Why did she have Pepper in the first place? She always disliked dogs. ("Too messy.") The most compelling explanation: Pepper was a gift from my father, who loved dogs. Trouble was, for whatever reason, my mother had ceased to love him.

There's a more teasing possibility: my mother brought both Pepper and me from Rockford, Illinois to

Calumet, Michigan at the same time. Granted, this is unlikely—her alone in a car on a long drive with a puppy and an infant. Yet a determined woman could have accomplished the deed. I was only left at my grandparents at such a young age as the result of great determination, among other things.

Damn the improbability. I like the spectacle of arriving in Calumet along with a dog. That is, I like it now. Now the scene is comic—Pepper and me each pissing away in the back seat or else yowling with various kinds of discomfort, while my mother wished she could just throw us both into Lake Superior, somewhere after she drove onto the Upper Peninsula, once the ferry from the Lower Peninsula landed.

And when so many long hours later she finally made it to Calumet? Oh, how I wish there was a photograph or two of that day. How would Gramps look? Granny? Best of all, my mother. No photos exist of an infant boy nestled in her arms. My imaginary photograph of that arrival day would reveal her sheer relief at last at being able to cast all manner of messy things out of obligatory reach.

But of course back then when both dog and infant were alive, the actuality must not have been so amusing—not even to Pepper. Maybe he bit me because he held me responsible for his displacement. And in a way, I was, since however the logic actually worked out among the adults he would never have fallen into my mother's clutches had she not given birth to me.

Poor Pepper. I'd like to believe he enjoyed a good life, often cavorting outside in a large, fenced yard, getting into occasional trouble in the garden, and never being punished by an older couple who cared for him or the child who tried to play with him. To the end, Pepper was just a dog, ever at the edge of the frame, never the reason for it having come into existence.

III.

CULTURE

Me with My Cap Pistol

Before Television

There used to be a popular radio show entitled, "Queen for a Day." The host, Jack Bailey, interviewed a succession of women about their woeful lives. The studio audience voted on them. Most woeful got to be queen, and was regaled with gifts, as the audience—and millions in the "radio audience"—cheered.

Granny & I were among the millions. She loved the mid-day show. I loved listening to it with her, beside a big brown Philco radio (the size of a nineteen-inch television set today) set atop a special wooden stand. We would pull up our chairs close at the start of the show. Granny usually knit. Sometimes I held the yarn for her.

What else did we listen to? In the evening, I remember "The Shadow Knows," mainly for the gleeful cackle of these words by the announcer at the beginning. (In answer to the question, "Who knows what evil lurks in the hearts of men?") I don't remember more. Radio listening appears in my imagination now as a very private, not to say intimate, conversation. It scarcely seems public, or cultural, at all.

What formed me as a cultural subject? If the traditions of "the old country" shaped my grandparents, they never used this phrase or spoke of anything directly. I attended church as well as "served" (as the idiom went) but I wasn't a member of any group, and, though I sang during Mass at all the requisite times, I didn't belong to a choir.

In the ethnic brew that was Calumet in the 40s, which group rated the highest? Poles must have been pretty high. Not as high as the Germans. But high. Certainly much higher than the Finns. "Dirty Finns," people used to say. To me, Finns were mythical creatures. I didn't know any. Presumably Finns were dirty because they had no culture.

There were no musical instruments in our house. Gramps didn't play any. Granny didn't either. We did have an old Victrola cabinet in the dining room. You had to use a handle to wind it up each time you played a thirty-three-and-a-third record. In my memory, this was not often. If there was music to the lives of my grandparents, it must have vanished by the time I came to live with them.

Nights were quiet. Gramps read the paper and went to bed early. Granny talked to me about this and that—mostly that. She wasn't a rich anecdotal source, either of her mother or my mother. Any culture from my grandparents' house—apart from that implicit in the Catholic faith—I received from outside.

But if my experience is any indication, in the 40s the family unit remained so secure from the outside, in whatever form other than radio, that the outside didn't really exist. (In a town such as Calumet, the newspaper was delivered to your door.) The singular exception was television, which began to be broadcast in the United States in 1947.

I was six years old in 1947. If within five more years thousands of Americans had acquired a television set for their homes, none I was in had. In my memory, I only saw a single television set by the time I left

Calumet, and this was one in the public realm: a bowling alley in Houghton.

Houghton was some ten miles away. The first time we went to see it constituted a special trip. And there "the television" was: a glassy box-like object placed high above the eating section of the bowling alley. For all it meant to me, the screen could have been just as well showing a test pattern as Howdy Doody. The great thing was to behold the set itself, under the sign of a Vision.

I don't remember who took me—some friend's father, I think—but Granny wasn't along. Had she seen the television, could she possibly have imagined how soon it would displace the centrality of radio? Her beloved "Queen for a Day" was a perfect example, since the television version first appeared in 1956, a year before the radio version ended, and then ran until 1964. What would Granny have thought had she lived to see this development?

I'd like to believe she'd have ignored the television show, and just ceased being interested in Jack Bailey once the radio show was no more. Radio itself to her must have retained at least some of the character of an older Polish culture, which, though no longer communal, continued to be ultimately oral in nature. Listening possessed the character of ritual. The Philco, with a special doily on top, was a shrine.

And what of American culture itself? By 1947, not to say 1952, it had become widely manufactured. And yet not only was it not necessarily received passively by its audience, if Granny is any example. (Or even me.) Culture was still felt to be local. Even national productions could be made anywhere. I distinctly remember our incredulity when one year we learned that a show of

"Queen for a Day" was actually going to be broadcast from the Copper Country.

However, "Queen for a Day" was regularly broadcast from the Moulin Rouge Theater in the faraway, mythical land of Hollywood. The announcer said so. Did such a place actually exist? In Calumet, who knew? In a sense, who cared? For listeners like Granny, it sufficed that a favorite show was transmitted. To be concerned from where would be like asking where your knitting needles were made.

Fast forward a few years. Late one morning, after I moved to Los Angeles with my mother, we chanced to drive by a corner of Sunset & Vine streets. There suddenly was the Moulin Rouge! And the day's hopeful audience for "Queen for a Day, all queued up! Although it might still have been for the radio show rather than the television show, I must have dimly realized that now I was a cultural subject of an entirely sort. What sort? I would no longer be able to figure it out by listening to the radio.

Comics

Childhood gives us objects to which we become more passionately attached than any in our lives. These are our toys. Almost anything will do if we choose or chance to invest enough play in it. As a boy, I must have had my share of dump trucks, rubber balls, and wooden animals. It's a source of pain to me now that I can't recall a one. The irony of our attachment to our toys is that in time all of them prove dispensable.

I used to play marbles. It seems to me now that I liked the smooth texture of each one more than the smack of one into another. "Marbles" to me is the name of a substance or a shape rather than the name of a game. I didn't play marbles with anybody so much as I collected them. Nothing like the sound of a full bag of marbles jiggling in a cloth bag, as if to protect against the fear of being somebody "who didn't have all his marbles."

Come to think of it, this might explain one toy I do remember: a little canon. It was a heavy metal object. You could spring-load it with a tiny canon ball and then propel the ball a few feet. It drove adults crazy when I did this. So of course I continued to do it. Probably somebody eventually took the canon away from me. I missed loading that little ball, which must have been connected in my mind with tether balls or basketballs.

But if toys are fantasy objects for children that enable them to act out either an imaginary or an incipient role in the world, then my important toys had to consist of something not normally considered toys at all: comic books. For as far back as I can remember, I collected them–bought, traded, read, and stored them. Everything about comic books appealed to me.

By comparison, the train set I once had? Just one day left aside for good. I received it as a gift. (From Uncle John?) But I was never interested in distinguishing boxcars from coal dump cars or watching the searchlight car chug around track that I had carefully laid. And so it went with all of the less elaborate or expensive of my toys. On some particular day I left them all aside, sooner or later. Only the comics remained, stacked in boxes.

What was my exact relation to these comics? It's hard to describe accurately. For example, it wasn't to aspire to some fantasy of totality, such as the title character in *Edwin Mullhouse* (1972), in Steven Millhauser's beautifully realized novel of childhood. When Edwin discovers two missing issues, he's anguished beyond the power of his mock-biographer to describe it. "Sadly he spread out on his bed, in two neat rows, the twenty-two comic books that should have been twenty-four." Edwin suspects a new friend of having stolen the missing issues.

"It was as if," we read, [the friend] "had taken from him a piece of his past, making his life henceforward resemble a piece of a jigsaw puzzle from which a piece is missing. So that in the center of a billowing white sail you see a piece-shaped hole, from which the dark green table hideously shows." But my relation to comics wasn't quite like this. I didn't care about owning complete sets— which is probably the reason why I didn't particularly care for jigsaw puzzles.

Instead, my contact with comics seemed to express some desire for accumulation itself. Comic books were cheap and plentiful in the 40s. Although I liked "E.C" comics best—something about the gruesome stories or the ironic twists—I bought them all, from Captain Marvel to Donald Duck. (I was especially amused by Donald's proto-capitalist uncle, Scrooge McDuck.) A kind of sweet promiscuity attends my memory of my relation to comic books. It seemed I just liked to be around them, and I didn't much care which ones. Missing issues didn't pain me. Not having a fresh one to read did. Or, sometimes, not having just one to hold in my hand.

I only possess half a dozen or so photographs of myself during the years I lived in Calumet. My favorite shows me, at age seven or eight, sitting in a sofa chair in our living room. The dining room, with a glass cabinet, is just visible through a doorway. In my hands is what I always remember as a book. I remember a book because comic books have meant nothing to me for decades. Books have. I'm a college professor of literature. I cite books such as *Edwin Mullhouse* as if they are old friends.

But in fact what I hold in my hands in this photo is a comic book. Perhaps not even that, because the pages—each one open—are too large; it's more like a coloring book. What? The boy in this photo looks so serious, not to say somber—with the front of his thick hair slicked way back, the wide collar of his shirt arranged over his jacket, and the fold of his pants without a wrinkle. How could he not be reading a real *book*?

Of course perhaps he was, behind the camera. The boy is dressed too formally. He's performing the role of "reader" so self-consciously that what he's reading must be made to appear eminently visible. Surely this is not so much a photograph of the boy as he was to himself— solitary, ruminative—as a construction of him for the benefit of adults, to whom he appears proper and respectable.

I must have read real books–the sort on which Classic Comics were based. I just don't remember any. (It always amazes me to read autobiographies where the author casually details his or her earliest reading—everything from British children's classics to French romantics or Russian realists.) Now I can guess why: the comic books that I do remember in bulk functioned to keep me at a distance from the adult world that took the photograph of me.

In my comic world I was effectively free to shore up objects (they happened to be made of paper) over against something. What? Say a primal loss. I didn't confront this loss directly. The purpose of accumulation was to prevent this, or defer it. Granted, not any thing would have sufficed. Texts were best; you can see that the boy in the above photo, whatever else, is not a social creature. Comics—cheap in several different senses—were best of all.

Guns

Everybody hunted in the Upper Peninsula. Every man, that is, or man-to-be. But there was at least one exception: me. Gramps didn't hunt deer. I did accompany him once to shoot partridge. No luck. The forest was confusing, the birds were elusive, the gun was heavy—you name it. Hunting just didn't "take" with me. That's the easiest explanation.

I wound up with a B-B rifle anyway. A gift from Gramps? Carl? Certainly not Rudy; he wore natty coats and a flashy fedora. Rudy was an urban figure. There was nothing urban about Calumet. (Or anywhere else in the Upper Peninsula; maybe Rudy was from Detroit.) You sort of confirmed it either by having a gun or aspiring to have a gun. A B-B rifle was a starter gun.

Alas, there were no starter animals, except maybe squirrels. So I duly took my B-B gun out in the woods and pulled the trigger in the general direction of squirrels. Once I hit one! I may have been more startled (if not pained) than the squirrel, who scurried up a tree. That was enough "hunting" for me. Mostly, I just liked to cock the gun or load B-B's from a little red capsule, which resembled a shotgun shell.

My memory of a cap pistol is far more vague. I did have one, and shot off strips of caps like any other kid. But the imaginary attachment I might have formed to this pistol is only recoverable now from the stray example of a single black-and-white photograph. I don't know how I happen to have it. I don't know who took it. Most crucially, I don't know why anybody took it. Was I particularly enamored of this pistol?

You can hardly see it in the picture, since my body is so erect and stiff it seems to absorb into it the fact that my left hand holds a gun waist-high. It's a "pose." But how derived? My shirt seems to be a clue. It's some sort of "Western" shirt, with studded buttons, slanted pockets, and a gingham pattern cut over the shoulders and repeated at the cuffs. Although I'm not wearing boots and I don't have a hat, I'm a cowboy!

When is the last American generation of American kids who grew up modeling themselves on cowboys? (Or cowgirls.) It wasn't the 40s. If we had Gene Autry or Roy Rodgers, based on serials and movies as well as radio, television was readying new shows for the 50s and 60s featuring different variations of venerable heroes. Meanwhile, my own relation to Westerns must have been pure fantasy.

Perhaps it effectively replaced a hunting identity more appropriate to local circumstances. I may not have intended this to be the case. But it became so anyway. Or at least it seems to me no accident now that I possess a photo of a nine year-old cowboy holding a pistol in a deadpan stick-'em-up position rather than a photo of a nine-year-old hunter standing beside a dead deer in a proud I-got-'em-in-one-shot position.

I'm not quite certain how the face of the hunter should look. The face of my cowboy suggests a stone-cold killer. Although dressed like a cowboy, maybe inwardly I feel like the hero of an urban crime drama. How many of these movies had I seen? Enough to be actively shaped by them? Film noir was big in the 40s. How much made it as far as the Upper Peninsula, which was as remote—culturally as well as geographically—as anywhere in the United States?

A long-standing secret belief: had I remained in Calumet, I could easily have become a young hoodlum. Already, I smoked. More generally, my grandparents couldn't really exercise much control. Granny spoiled me. Gramps never disciplined me. Away from home, I had fallen into, well, young versions of the sort of people who comprise, say, the rustlers in a Western or the punks in a detective story. Although nobody engaged much in violence, there was nothing to prevent crime. The kids I hung around with stole things as a matter of course, and all of them were familiar with guns, either because they hunted, or, like me, fancied themselves cowboys.

My incipient criminal future was brought to a halt by one incident. I must have been eight or so when it happened. By this time stealing had become so routine I was ripe to become careless—and more ambitious. Heretofore my friends and I stole mostly from small corner groceries. This day another kid and I decided to hit the big Woolworth's on Fifth Street. To me, the attraction was a wall-size rack of magazines and comics at the front entrance.

He stuffed a few comics into his jacket, then wandered off, I was content with the comics. We were both grabbed by the manager before we got out to the street. He marched us to the rear of the store, up some stairs, and onto two chairs in his office, whereupon he called the police. It seemed like this was happening in a movie! Especially when a cop actually arrived—a real policeman!—and duly deposited us in his car.

"You're going to jail," he said, driving away, "unless you promise not to steal again." "We promise, we promise!" My friend, though, made one mistake. We had each emptied our jackets of the comics. But he had kept a really nice shiny plastic revolver. Fearing he might be frisked when we arrived at the jail, he took it out of his pants and stuffed it into the back seat. After we stopped, the cop frisked the back seat instead of frisking him.

Discovering the gun really made him angry. He proceeded to take us inside the jail and show us some empty cells. They were frightening. We swore up and down never to steal again. I don't remember what my friend said to explain hiding the revolver. I just kept pleading, "Please don't tell my grandmother, she has a weak heart." Maybe this was a line I had heard at the movies. But I believed it. What if Granny could die because of me!

The cop let us go with a warning. Granny never learned I had been, er, "arrested." It seems now like a happy ending. Just as happy, albeit in a more complicated way, is the story I can tell myself now: my life of crime—attested to by a partner who was already stealing guns—was cut short at the comic book stage. Even though already filled by movie fantasies, it seems finally my head was between the pages of a book. Own a gun? I would rather read about people who did.

Movies

She was soft, blonde, and scantily clad. Tarzan didn't love her. (Tarzan loved only Jane.) But I did. Or at least she stirred feelings in me that no other girl I ever saw on the screen ever did. I don't remember the plot; for some reason, Tarzan must have rescued her, since he was always rescuing people. I don't remember her name, and I never again saw either the movie or the actress who played her. But I've never forgotten this particular delicate jungle goddess. The best love is the first one, especially if it's impossible.

Could this woman have appeared in a serial? It's quite possible. My first filmic years coincided with some of the glory years for Hollywood serials on screen, after they emerged from their radio days in the 30s. At the Calumet Theater, I saw every serial that came through, from Tarzan to Dick Tracy, Captain Video through Sky King, Buck Rodgers and Flash Gordon, and how can I forget Blonde, with Dagwood Bumpstead. I loved 'em all.

Some of these serials, though, were either so poorly made or else so artificially plotted that even we kids laughed at them. Flash Gordon I especially remember, with sets as plausibly futuristic as my back yard and villains as menacing as a popcorn box under the seat. We loved to laugh, in the right or wrong places, it scarcely mattered, just as we thrilled to squirm at suspenseful moments or bounce up and down at exciting ones.

These serials must largely explain why I can hardly recall any specific feature films. Going to see a movie in the 40s meant expecting to see all sorts of other things besides a feature film: cartoons, newsreels, and serials. Nothing could be farther from "cinema" as we now know it. Compared to today, a movie screen then resembled a television screen, featuring a variety of visual material. And yet, especially with the curtain that lifted before anything was shown, a movie theater then was also partially modeled on the music hall that preceded it.

Moreover, the changes of heroes and their narratives from radio (or comic books) into screen (and then comic books) approximate Ovid in their transformations and mutations. I didn't prefer reading comics to watching movies. I liked both, as a function of the relay between the one and the other. In the same sense, serials—fifteen or twenty minutes long, over the course of twelve to fifteen episodes—whetted your appetite for feature length-movies. I was hooked.

Now I can only remember two movies, each for their highly emotional effect. One was a Lassie movie. The first one, *Lassie Come Home*? Probably not, since I was only two years old when the movie was released. It must have been a later one in the Lassie cycle—the radio show began in 1946—where Lassie is killed. I sobbed on our couch after getting home. Granny tried to comfort me. I was inconsolable.

The other movie was *The Thing*. It terrified me. I have a distinct memory of bolting from my seat at one particularly scary point and running up the aisle into the lobby. Is this really true? *The Thing* was released in 1951. In 1951 I turned ten. Ten seems to me pretty old to be so afraid (especially if you smoke and have already been arrested). But I believe I was once so afraid, and now the only apology I can plead is that I enjoyed it.

To have such responses is why I went to be movies each week—the Calumet Theater changed once a week—along with everybody else. I didn't go with Gramps or Granny. I went by myself (the theater was only a block or so away) and just met other kids there, each of whom left home alone just as I had. We bought popcorn or Milk Duds. (Both if you had enough money.) We sprawled in our seats. (Each one sort of creaked when you pulled it down.) We howled at Micky Mouse cartoons. We were silent through the Pathe World News. Soon it was time for Johnny Weissmuller (say) to give his familiar full-throated bellow as he swung across one vine to another, as Dagwood Bumpstead could never dream of doing.

Were movies for me a kind of "escape?" Sure. Easy enough to say if your perspective is what you escape from. Calumet in the 40s had plenty to escape from, beginning with the snow bank just a few feet from the ticket window. But "escapism" is harder to clarify if your perspective is what you escape into. In effect, I escaped into everything from the experience of sexual desire to the prospect of death. That these things were a form of play—if you asked me, I wouldn't have said any were "real"—only intensified their power.

The power was already heightened by being a collective phenomenon. Of course it's still available today in the Cineplex. But it's available over against the knowledge that you could just as easily—or more easily—be at home watching a DVD. In the 40s of course no such knowledge was conceivable. Part of the reason you went to a movie in the first place was to be among other people. Either they experienced the same emotions you did. Or else your own emotions—however different—got caught up in theirs.

There was only one I had that separated me, one thing I knew that made me the envy of my own experience, if only I could have had it. I don't remember when I learned what I knew. Probably somewhere between *Lassie* and *The Thing*. It seems to me somebody (Aunt Eleanor?) chanced to make an offhand remark. The remark was this: my father had been the manager of the Calumet Theater. The manager! Imagine just what this meant! I imagined it: his son, me, could have gotten in each week free!

So where was my father now, when I needed him? (No matter that I always had money to go to the movies.) How had fate—I never questioned God—been so cruel as to deny me a father? This was far worse than denying me a jungle goddess. Or was this father of mine as much a fantasy as the goddess? It would take a lot longer than a succession of weeks to figure this out. Meanwhile, movies seemed to console me, as if the succession of a new episode or plot each week would somehow substitute for the same old story which never appeared.

SOCIETY

Sports

In 1952 a Detroit Tigers pitcher, Virgil Trucks, did something no one else has done since: pitch two no-hitters in a single season. The first was on May 15. The second was on August 25. The exact dates surprise and unsettle me to discover. By this time, I was nearly eleven. Granny had not yet died. I had not left Calumet. And yet she was soon to die and I was soon to leave. So why do I have such a vivid memory of walking alone along a street, listening to my little transistor radio to Trucks's second no-hitter, and just about bursting into tears of relief when the last out was recorded?

To put the same question in the form of a declarative statement: my memory of sports is a solitary one. No football. (I was on the team for a couple years in high school.) No basketball. (I was a starting guard during my sophomore year.) No baseball. (I could never hit a pitch.) Hockey only in the form of pick-up games on the street, which always turned into what adults termed "roughhousing." Playing tether ball in the schoolyard didn't seem to count as a "sport" any more than swinging on the "Jungle Jim" set.

Once I had a student who told me why she switched from basketball to volleyball. She liked being part of the team effort in volleyball—everybody slapping hands or clapping backs after each serve or return, no matter what the result. By contrast, basketball effort was too individualistic. Her explanation shocked me. Sports seemed to me all individual effort. But this not only meant I was a male. It meant I had the childhood athletic experience—the center of much of the rest of my experience—of a solitary male.

My solitude came out best in baseball. I was strictly a fan. I loved the Detroit Tigers. I never saw a game. (In my dim memory, we only drove down to the Lower Peninsula once to visit some friends of either Gramps or Granny in Detroit; the city was a blur—too big for me to take in.) Is it possible I never even dreamed that one day I would see the Tigers play? But how was this possible? Everybody knows that such a prospect is the stuff of a boy's dreams. How could I not have hoped one day to get the autograph of Walt Dropo or Hal Newhauser?

One reason: baseball cards. I collected them. Mostly Bowman, a bubble gum company. (Topps didn't begin until 1952.) Not only Tigers or American League teams but National League teams, too. I collected baseball cards, I suppose, for the same reason I collected comic books: to construct a fantasy world whose principle of accumulation kept the actual world both manageable and at bay. But it seems to me now there was one significant difference. A good part of collecting baseball cards consisted of trading them with other kids.

Of course you traded comics as well. But not so quickly and systematically, at least in my experience. The point of the cards was to get hold of certain players, or, better, a big star, a Willie Mays or Micky Mantle. There was nothing comparable to this with respect to comics. Also, you tried to get an entire team; therefore, baseball cards were indispensable, whereas a comic book, once read, you could trade away or get rid of. These differences meant that collecting baseball cards, in sum, became a social practice. They got you into society and kept you there.

Granted, the society was kids-only, beneath the world of adults and based on single-minded intensities that the adults could not sustain. Nonetheless, baseball card collection supplied its own conventions, its own vocabulary, and its own values, as well as its own population. Somebody who had a card you wanted seemed to be a potential friend. Somebody else who got that card instead felt like an enemy. Alliances and counter-alliances were formed daily at the schoolyard. Hierarchies existed. Certain kids were celebrated for their prowess.

I don't know if I was one. Possibly I was better than most, but not as clever or single-minded as the best. Twenty years ago I sold two shoeboxes-full of cards. They were all I had managed to retain. Almost every card—from the period, 1949-52—was in pretty good condition. There was even a "mint" Willie Mays! A collector offered me a thousand dollars for both boxes, cash. It felt like selling my childhood. Then I remembered my board game. I once played it remorselessly, for hour upon hour, all by myself.

It was actually a basketball game. The ball was a ping-pong ball. You set it on a spring, from either end of the court, and tried to make a basket on the other end, by pulling back a little tin lever and releasing it with the right touch. But my game was baseball. So I worked out a system that changed baskets into hits, and then I computed batting averages of individual players. Some of them were contemporary ones, including most Tigers, but many players were older ones. I tried to make my averages square with their actual ones. So Ty Cobb always came out on top.

Oh, how I loved playing! I had a special brown spiral notebook, with pages and pages of box scores to imaginary games. Some of them were World Series games! The reader of American fiction will inevitably recall Robert Coover's novel, *The Universal Baseball Association, J. Henry Waugh, Prop* (1971), wherein a man fantasizes into existence an entire eight-team league, complete with biographies of players and season-long narratives. But Waugh is fifty-seven. I was seven—or eight, nine, ten. Moreover, Waugh is utterly lost in his own world.

I was lost in mine. But only during special times, when, it appears, kids strive wholly to realize themselves as kids while at the same time they play out in imagination a mastery they are not yet prepared to live in society. Finally, my own world remained continuous with the actual world, or so it seemed to have worked out. In both worlds Virgil Trucks pitched while Ty Cobb hit and a kid in my class named Richard was smarter than me but I had more baseball cards than he did.

Gender

I didn't care for guns. I didn't play sports. I did play "King of the Hill." Girls didn't. I did smoke. Girls never did. (Once I was with Aunt Eleanor in a restaurant and she whispered for me to look at a woman across the room. "Can you see she's smoking?") But how was I to know—no, how was I to be *confident* that I was a boy who would one day be a man? I never had such confidence, or at least I never did if two of my clearest, most acute memories are any indication. Each one involves death. In one, I almost died. In the other, I did.

Occasionally, Gramps used to take us to Copper Harbor, the tip of the Upper Peninsula. There's no beach there, just rocks. Even if there was a beach, the water of Lake Superior is pretty cold. What you can find, though, are little inlets where some sand accumulates on each side of the tiny stream, and the bottom is not entirely rocky. One Sunday (it must have been) we went there. But to me there was one problem. Granny (it must have been) made me put on a girl's single-piece swimsuit.

I can still feel its scratchy texture. I can still see its color, black. What I can't explain is why I was forced to wear the suit in the first place. Couldn't my grandparents have afforded a boy's swimsuit? Didn't they see how upset I was to have to wear a girl's? Did they think I was "cute" in it? How old was I this day? I can't remember. But I was old enough to care about being a boy, not a girl. You could tell the difference because each "gender" (a word nobody used) had its own swimsuit.

I almost drowned in mine. One moment I was playing in the inlet. The next moment I slipped. Water closed over me. My mouth bubbled. A few more moments and someone was lifting me out. I woke up laid out on the sand with water squirting out of my mouth and ears. A man was squeezing me, hard. Lots of people were gathered around me. It was very confusing and scary. However, what I remember most of all is tremendous embarrassment.

Everybody could see I was dressed like a girl. Almost as bad, I can understand now, I was in a "feminine" position, unable to fend for myself and having to be rescued by a man. At the time, I was only conscious of the suit. Or, I suppose, conscious of a "self," namely me, who was in the suit. It was as if I had been discovered cross-dressing! Only I was only five or six years old and it wasn't my fault!

Tempting from the present perspective to play Freudian: secretly, I wanted to drown. My fall was deliberate—an infantile suicide attempt! Or else, more subtly, I enacted a "fall" into gender, only it was the wrong gender, and so I was moved to protest! This sort of reasoning is fun to engage in now. But it was terrible to have to endure the experience of it then. The terror is not that I almost drowned. It's that I almost drowned as a girl.

Most likely, I was so spoiled—how not to use the passive voice?—that even by age six I was effectively "unmanned." I had become what was surely known then as a "mama's boy." Was it worse—softer, more inexorable—to become a grandmother's boy? How to *resist* becoming spoiled? Or does this idiom express an assumption that you can't resist—or else you wouldn't be spoiled? Furthermore, if you're spoiled, you fail to be subject to social pressures or constructions, which limit the spoilage, if not its emotional damage.

For all I know now, I must have been a scandal to such society as comprehended my existence. Easy to envision the discourse: Granny loved me, yes, yes. So she spoiled me. What could anyone do to prevent this? Very little. After all, she was an old woman, and, well, she loved me. Something might have been added at this point about my parents, to the effect that I was very much like an abandoned or orphaned child., poor thing. "No wonder he's spoiled." And so on, while I continued—mostly quite content—as a victim.

Yet it wasn't quite this simple. I also colluded with my victimization and there was a stark symbol for my collusion: a bear. Just a commonplace cloth thing. It's probably very important to know how I came by this toy. I can't remember. What I do remember is that for years I chewed on it, knotting up strips of cloth when they came loose, so I could chew some more. I remember that everybody—including Granny—was upset that I clung to this bear. It was dirty. (I had to hide it in various places so nobody could take it.) It was childish.

What some who visited us may have said in addition is that the bear was female. I had a doll! Just because it wasn't in the form of a girl didn't mean it wasn't a girlish toy. Boys don't play with dolls! I did. So I couldn't be a boy—I wouldn't be safe in the male gender—unless I stopped playing with this doll. But evidently I didn't want to stop. I clung to this bear as if my life depended on it. Do you have to have a gender in order to have a life?

It fell to Uncle Carl to solve this particular dilemma for me. He acted the day of Granny's funeral. In my memory the deed happened in the following way: we returned home and Uncle Carl headed straight for the victrola. He knew I hid the bear there. When I saw him, I wailed in protest. When he got hold of the bear, I grabbed it. But Carl was a grown man. I was not yet eleven years old. He easily jerked the bear from me. And that was the end of the doll.

The fact that I can't recall exactly what he did with it is, I believe, an indication of the trauma of its disappearance, like Granny, from my life. It almost seems too neat. I lost the bear, Granny, and my presence in the female gender simultaneously. Sometimes your own experience embarrasses you. And it may be that insofar as gender is concerned, its decisive moments are based either on embarrassment or its immanent shadow. It took me too long to become a boy. First I had to die as a girl.

Food

Pasties. In the 40s, these half-moon-shaped Cornish meat pies hadn't become the U.P. icon they are today. You didn't see advertising posters and billboards announcing the best restaurants in which to eat them. Instead, pasties were usually cooked as they had always been, in the home. When I was growing up, I couldn't have imagined eating a pasty in a restaurant. It would have been like trying to imagine different people each night at our kitchen table eating a pasty Granny had cooked.

For a long time I thought pasties were Polish. Like us. Come to find out, each of Calumet's other major immigrant groups—Finns, Serbs, Croats, Italians—either claimed the dish for themselves or else had similar pies in their own traditions that could be made to become pasties. It was like the Catholicism claimed by each individual ethnic church (a few of them already closed when I was a kid). But if I only had a limited experience of religion, I had an even more limited experience of food.

I remember Granny's pasties best. They were so good I even ate the vegetables and onions inside, along with the diced meat. Often, I helped her make pasties. This way I got to eat the baking dough, raw. After she rolled out the dough, I broke off little strips and popped them in my mouth. There must have been a few times when I consumed all the dough before she could pour the ingredients onto it, wrap it over them, and pinch the edges into a crust. If so, I'll bet Granny just laughed and kneaded some more dough from her bowl.

What else did we eat? Is it possible that I don't remember anything? It is, because I don't. Whatever it was, what I do remember is that I didn't like it, except for the deserts, especially pies. (Pie was a sort of pasty reborn as a sweet.) That is, I was permitted to refuse pretty much anything, and I did. Or else if some attempt was made—probably more by Gramps than Granny—to make me eat something, I'd just sneak it into my pockets and throw it out into the garden when nobody was looking.

Today I can't believe I actually did this. But I did. With the singular exception of pasties, my experience of food when I was a child was based on rejection, not consumption. I used to open the screen door, stand on the wooden steps out back, and heave all sorts of food—especially vegetables—as far as I could. Sometimes I'd wad up bread just to see how far it could travel. The garden took up fully half the yard. It was dense with lots of leafy things—tomato plants, lettuce. If the birds didn't get what I threw away, the ground would somehow absorb it.

In fact, who cleaned up the garden? Not me, anyway. More importantly, who knew besides Gramps and Granny how shamelessly I rejected food? Neighbors? But in the person of a kindly old couple, the Shafers, who lived next to us on the side opposite the garden and probably felt little more about me than that I was a "nice little boy," nobody probably knew anything about my behavior. Aunt Eleanor perhaps? Uncle Carl, certainly.

After all, Carl knew about my bear. Yet it seems even Uncle Carl couldn't force me to eat once I refused.

A child's world is such a small one! The more mine threatened somehow to expand into the larger social realm, the more I must have willed it to contract. Food wasn't a substance. It was a battleground. To me, food didn't exist for sustenance or pleasure. It existed for power. And what did I take myself to control by refusing to eat? My own growth, I suppose—not only as a boy but as a nascent member of society, which consisted, in turn, of people at dining tables who "consumed" each other—talking, sharing—when they ate together. But my little world finally consisted of me alone, and I tried to keep it this way for as long as I could. Granny helped me, bless her, and, albeit more indirectly, so did Gramps. The strength of their parental energies must have been largely depleted—or exhausted—by the time I came into their lives. They could feed me. But at most they could nourish me only up to that moment that I got up from our table and opened the back door.

When I came to live with my mother in Los Angeles after Granny died, she enrolled me in a military school. I boarded there during the week. Three meals a day to six cadets at assigned tables, each presided over by a table leader and served by a special group of other cadets, who ate among themselves beforehand. During my second year at the school, I became one of these servers. Perhaps I had contrived to be one in order to try to continue to exercise my old Calumet will over food, having already gotten into trouble with at least two table leaders. The first one insisted that I eat tomatoes. The second insisted that I eat fish.

One day my fellow servers and I sat down to dinner. The dish was a surprise: venison. Venison was yet another thing I refused to eat in Calumet. (It just appeared "strange.") For some reason, though, this day I not only tried to eat it but to wield some authority about its culture over my fellows. In fact, I knew as little about deer as they did. But they didn't know this—and, for once, my exotic Calumet origins might pay off. At one point I opined thus: "Oh, venison. That's all we eat in Michigan."

Fatal words! One of the servers was a kid named Howe. Bigger than the rest of us, he had a terribly pimple-ridden face and a mouth that emitted strange clicking noises when he periodically skipped as he walked. I didn't like Howe. He didn't like me. My boast was a boon for him. Howe immediately began repeating my words. The rest of the servers picked up the chant. "That's all we eat in Michigan." I was humiliated during the rest of the dinner. Far worse, over the course of the next few days, other kids would chant, "That's all we eat in Michigan," when they saw me.

A day or two more and I openly confronted Howe. We proceeded to have a brief scuffle until we were separated. After this, his mockery stopped and so did that of others. If I hadn't learned anything more about food since Calumet by this time, I learned something now. You may be able to eat or not to eat anything you want, but you can't just say anything you want about it. The closed, precious world of the family is not equivalent to the open world of society, where you have to be prepared, as we say, to "eat" your words. That day I should have either kept my mouth shut or else told my fellows all about pasties.

Sex

Once during one of those timeless childhood afternoons when there was nothing much to do, a group of us kids were lounging in an alley. We fell to talking about sex. Since we didn't know what we were talking about, everybody had an idea. On one point we were all in agreement: each time a man and a woman had "intercourse"—did we actually use this word or did we say, "fucked?"—the woman would have a baby. Suddenly somebody mentioned a family in which there were eight kids. This meant that the mother and father had "done it" *eight times*! Haw, haw. We weren't just a bunch of bored, ignorant kids anymore.

Except of course we were. How to locate the precise presence of sex in our lives? In one respect, there wasn't any. We were too young, and only vaguely aware of older kids who paired off in dim, intense ways. Others my age may have been less vaguely aware of sex than me because of their parents. My own grandparents abided in a realm effectively beyond sexuality, and, although I must had some inchoate inkling of what went on behind the curtain at Sego's, I would probably have believed it if you would have told me Gramps went there to eat special pasties.

In another respect, though, sex existed. Or at least, mysteries existed, and "sex" was the name for one of these mysteries, if not for all of them combined. On another afternoon, I have a memory of a kid appearing in the street and waving around something in his hand. Nobody wanted to go near him. When I got near, I saw a white, cottony thing with red spots on it. The kid said it was blood. It came from girls. It seemed at "special times" they bled! During these times something had to be used to absorb the blood. This thing was called, "Kotex." Ugh!

You didn't learn about such things in school. And yet, school seems to me now to have been a sort of stage for the fitful production of all sorts of things I secretly wanted to learn about but couldn't, because the lighting was so poor, the sets minimal, and the actors—including me—unsure of their lines. Take Anita, the only schoolmate I remember having some sort of "special feeling" about. It was fourth grade. I was ready to win her heart. But there was one problem: Richard.

Richard was the smartest kid in the class, and he knew it. It's not clear to me if Anita, who was also pretty smart, really liked Richard. But she could often be seen in his company. This was enough to stir my jealousy. (Or, for all I remember, create my desire for Anita in the first place.) Now what to do? I had no lines to speak. I never heard any. (Most of the movies were about cowboys, gangsters, and soldiers.) The only thing to do was to lead with what I had: comic books. Richard didn't seem to care about them. Maybe Anita did. I have a distinct memory of visiting her home with a handful.

Then I don't remember what happened, except that I didn't get the girl. Whether or not Anita consented to accept my comic offering that day, she continued with Richard. It seems to me I was less hurt than puzzled. Had I done something wrong? Had Richard done something right? Could Anita somehow be to blame? Should I have brought her Kotex instead of comics? Of such questions does childhood sexuality consist. I'm not sure a naked picture of a woman or a steamy novel would have clarified anything.

This failed affair with Anita is connected in my mind with an incident that happened one winter morning across the street from my house. The usual noisy stream of kids on their way to Morrison was unsettled by something Arnold was doing. Everybody knew Arnold was "strange." Nobody used the word, "retarded." This particular morning it seemed that some kids had persuaded Arnold to open his zipper and let his dick (that's what we called it) dangle. Much hilarity ensued. Arnold himself seemed to be enjoying it.

My response was uncharacteristically aggressive: I rushed across the street, cursed the laughing kids, and told Arnold to put his dick back in his pants. Did I really do this? I believe my memory is correct. But why did I do this? Now, the only reason that sounds true is that, once more, sex had appeared in my conscious experience under the guise of something shameful. If you asked me what was shameful about it, I couldn't have said. Perhaps I would have banished the very question; the fact that sex should be kept hidden virtually constituted the nature of sex.

One of the first things my mother did for me when we got to Los Angeles was take me to meet Janet Leigh. I don't know how she arranged it. My mother worked as a manicurist in Beverly Hills. Probably one of her customers knew Janet Leigh, my favorite actress. In any case, one Sunday morning we drove down Wilshire Boulevard to an apartment house, and there Janet Leigh was in front of it, with her husband, Tony Curtis, who had his leg in a cast.

There was time enough for me to utter an abashed hello and to take her picture. Janet Leigh! A real Hollywood movie star! What would Ziggy think? I sent a copy of the picture to him, along with a description of the meeting. The explanation must have been smutty and sniggering. Given my attitude toward sex, how could it not be? Ziggy evidently wrote back in kind. My mother opened the letter and refused to let me read it.

Thus effectively ended my friendship with Ziggy, although it would probably have ended soon anyway, because Ziggy couldn't write very well. Once more, my life in Los Angeles was accomplished by the end of my life in Calumet. How not to feel that at least insofar as sex is concerned, the life well lost? Had I remained in Calumet, how long might I have gone on so ignorant of basic facts and so shadowed by childish fears? What sort of man would I have grown up to be? Easy—too easy—for me to wonder now that it might have been a man who had eight kids, joked about his wife with the boys at the bar, and went to bed secretly dreaming of having sex with Janet Leigh.

IV

Me Reading

George Gip

"Win one for the Gipper." This request is part of American sports lore, if not of our very language. It was of course supposedly spoken to Knute Rockne by George Gip, Notre Dame's first All-American football player, as he lay dying of pneumonia. The year was 1920. Twenty years later Ronald Regan played Gip in the movie. Poor Gip. With the movie, he became more legendary and perhaps less real. But not in the Upper Peninsula. Gip was born in Laurium, the seventh of eight children, and is buried there.

Laurium begins from the other side of the highway where Calumet ends. It's a little more than twice the size of Calumet, and is the site of the area Middle School as well as Calumet High School. In the 40s, once you finished 5th grade at Morrison you had to go to Laurium to begin the 6th grade. I could still walk to school, once I had to make the trip in fall of 1952, although now the distance between home and school was now far enough (a couple of miles) to amount to a wholesale redefinition of "school."

Morrison may as well have been an extension of home, it was so close. Maybe this is why I remember so much about home and so little of school. Laurium, though, was something else entirely. There were lots of kids I didn't know. Some of them were big. Was big worse than unknown? One thing for sure: this school had a saint: George Gip. Is it possible I'd never heard of Gip until I reached 6th grade?

As if to immediately remedy some vast ignorance, new kids were solemnly taken downstairs to stand before a glass case next to the gym. It was a veritable shrine devoted to Gip. There were plaques for his many records (mostly in baseball), pennants for his championships, newspaper accounts of his college stardom, and so on. We were meant to be awed and we were. And yet could it be that I wasn't quite as awed as I should have been?

It sounds like me—me, that is, as I grew up to be. I dislike piety. I accept authority grudgingly. I'm sarcastic. Even as young as I was in 1952, could I have made some irreverent remark as our Guide to Gip—some older kid—was droning on? Could either he or another kid—a football player, say—have heard me and taken offense? All I remember is that very soon after I began 6th grade there was a big kid who didn't like me and who was resolved to do me harm.

I was scared. This kid had friends. I had none. He and his friends had occasion. Either we all had a physical education class together or he and his friends could get hold of me anytime between classes. Already once they had dragged me to a sink, filled it with water, and tried to dunk me. I struggled free. What about the next time? What about having to walk to this new school every day and worry about what might happen to me?

It might sound nice to write that I sought solace from George Gip, standing in front of his shrine with head bowed and—and, well, silently praying either for his inspiration or his intercession. But this wouldn't be true. Whether or not I had ever heard of Gip before, I didn't feel the need of his spirit. I needed my own, and I wasn't sure I had what it took—whatever it was—to face this big, mean kid and his buddies.

Did it take the courage to fight? I hated fighting. Friends? Well, I still had Ziggy. (Ronnie seemed to have drifted away.) But Ziggy wasn't a fighter either. Brothers? Of course I had none. Perhaps, though, I began now to wonder for the first time how different my life would be if I had just one brother. Everybody else seemed to have one. Why not me? Why couldn't the security of home—as I believe I experienced it—be stretched to cover school?

As it turned out, it did. But not as I could have imagined. One sudden day Granny had a heart attack. She was taken to the hospital. Or else she was taken to the hospital and there she had a heart attack. I was never sure. Was I too shocked? Granny was the bedrock of my little world. It was inconceivable something could happen to her. Or was I too absorbed in my own problems—a new school, a sudden enemy? Probably some combination of both.

Then came a school day when I was called out of class. It must have been by the principal. Did he inform me I had to go home, because my grandmother had died? Or did he just inform me I had to go home, and then somebody else—presumably Gramps—would tell me why? Except for one thing, I can't be sure. Except for this thing, I can't even be sure that Granny had in fact died (and instead had only been taken to the hospital).

But I'm pretty sure I was informed that my grandmother had died because once I got up and left the classroom I remember the immediate sensation that I was never coming back to the school. I must have sensed the reason, although I doubt I could have voiced it. Now (I felt) I was free of that big kid and his friends. No more violence. I wouldn't have to be afraid of being dunked anymore.

And there was something else. On the basis of it I must not only have sensed I was never coming back to school but also that something momentous had happened—Granny had actually died. She wasn't just hospitalized. She was dead. How else could I have been certain that I was leaving the classroom for the last time? As I got my books and left, how else could I have felt something I'm ashamed to remember so clearly now: relief.

Mary

Mary wasn't my first love. Quite the reverse: I was her first love. It makes me inexpressibly sad to remember her. (I wouldn't be surprised if she doesn't remember me at all.) It's as if Mary embodies to me much of Calumet itself—its forlorn beauty, its secret resources, its promise, its loss.

Mary was the sister of a friend. I remember visiting their house more than once. The family lived across the railroad tracks. What did their father do? What ethnic background did he have? These were crucial Calumet questions then, although they didn't really matter very much—not even in Calumet—to a ten year-old kid.

Mary must have known me all her life. She was older than me—perhaps by as many as three years. How did she first exhibit some special interest? Was it during a time I visited to see her brother? I can't remember feeling any special interest in her, at least until it seemed clear she had some in me.

Then what? Once again, my memory draws its customary blank. Did Mary and I proceed to spend time together, away from other kids? Did we exchange tender words? Did we kiss? I don't believe any of this actually happened, although it's amusing, no, moving to imagine now that Mary might have wanted it to.

I write this because of her response to me after Granny's death. She was very concerned, worried, solicitous. I was actually leaving! Going to California to live! Me, Terry, the boy she knew—and now might never see again. How must he be feeling? California was as remote and unimaginable as Slovenia.

The night before I was scheduled to leave I remember now as if it were a movie. Suddenly Mary appeared at our back door—the same one outside of which I used to stand to throw food into the garden. She brought me a basket of cookies and fruit. She couldn't let me leave without saying good-bye one last time.

What words were on her lips to add? What words were on mine? Snow flurries danced in the air. We promised to write. Gramps growled at me to get back inside. Finally I had to close the door and Mary had to go. To write this now is to hear an unseen theater audience softly sobbing.

Mary really did write. I've misplaced one letter I saved. It always used to amaze me to read how astonishingly well-written this letter was. (Just the opposite of poor Ziggy's barely literate scrawl.) Mary was a smart girl. Perhaps at least in part she had identified with my sunny California future, which would most likely never be hers.

Maybe I deliberately misplaced the letter because it just pained me too sharply to have to realize anew how swiftly the correspondence dried up. Finally, Mary and I were still kids, with barely more to share than the immediate circumstances—friends, a fire down the street, next week's weather—of kids. Now we didn't have anything in the present to share. Now our present was past.

Who wrote last? I hope it was me. I don't even remember Mary's last name. It would be virtually impossible now to get hold of her, even if I wanted to.

What if she not only forgot all about me, even forgot that night when she brought me that basket? What if she went on to have eight kids, every single one of whom is now older than she and I were then?

In one of her first letters, Mary enclosed a photo of herself. I stare at it now as the very image of a long-vanished past. Mary remains a tall, rather chunky girl; in memory, she was simply "bigger than me." Mary's face looks lively, sharp, pretty; in memory, the first thing that comes to mind is that she wears glasses.

Mary is on a beach. It must be Lake Superior. Therefore it's windy. (Visible in the background are small whitecaps rolling in to shore.) Her short hair is blown and her arms rest stiffly at her sides as if she's cold. Mary is wearing three-quarter length pants and a cable-stitched sweater. She's smiling and she's standing firmly.

Could I have once reciprocated receiving this picture by sending Mary the one I took of Janet Leigh? If so, how crude! Yet I could have done so. Almost impossible for a kid from Calumet to go to California, no, to *Hollywood*, and not flaunt it. Indeed, it would almost be disappointing to friends left behind if this kid didn't flaunt it; nobody wanted to receive pictures of palm trees.

If so, though, could it even have been worse: upon receipt of the Janet Leigh photograph, Mary simply gave up the correspondence? After all, how could a thirteen or fourteen year-old girl compete with Janet Leigh? It's a measure of a lifetime—even if it's no consolation—to say that it's no competition now (if it ever was then). Mary's picture is inexpressibly more precious to me.

Just to try to express why anyway: the photograph allows an impossible past to appear visible. Some of the impossibility has to do with a relation that was never lived out and could never have been lived out. The rest has to do with a species of time abstracted from duration as well as circumstance. This time is past. But in the form of a beautiful young girl on a beach it looks as if it has yet to come into existence.

Flying Away

The two-photograph packet is stapled together. The front cover gives the photo shop as, Flanders Photo Finisher, P.O. Box 57, Waycross, Georgia. This means my Uncle John, who lived in Waycross, must have sent or given me the packet. He himself appears in one of the photos, which were both taken on the runaway before the plane took off to take me away from Calumet, after Granny died. You can read the name of the airline, Wisconsin Central.

Grouped in the first picture are Uncle Carl and his wife, their two kids, Gramps, my mother, and me. I never could figure out his wife, or even Carl for that matter; here, it's hard to tell if a faint smile either expresses or suppresses whatever he's feeling. Gramps, with his familiar black suit, vest, tie, and gray hat, looks exhausted and sad. Wearing a nicely cut three-quarter-length coat, in whose pockets I have my hands, I have my usual poker-face look. My hair needs to be combed.

My mother stands to one side of me and slightly behind, with one arm around me. She's attired in light waist-length coat, long dark skirt, and pumps. She's holding her purse in the other hand, and wearing white gloves. There's a kind of squint to her face. I don't know how to read this look. On the other side of her stands Carl, but not closely. The space between Carl Tobola and Martha Caesar marks the exact center of the picture.

Who took this picture? It must have been Uncle John, who appears at far left of the second photo, wearing a raincoat and his usual jovial aspect. Carl's smile is threatening to become broader, Gramps's face is even more downcast, and I now appear stricken. My mother looks the most different. Now far right, she blankly stands behind me, clutching her purse with both hands. Every curly hair is in place.

A familiar factual fog descends over each of these photographs. How much time passed, for example, between this moment—my last in the Upper Peninsula for the next forty years—and the day of Granny's death? What went into the construction of my departure? Had there been extensive discussion among Gramps, his two sons, and his daughter about my fate? Was there any disagreement? If so, who disagreed, and why?

Perhaps it was just immediately apparent to all that I could not remain with Gramps. Instead, I obviously had to leave, and live with my mother. Impossible for me not to speculate now that Carl—with two young kids of his own—had had his fill of me. John was a bachelor (much later I found out he was gay) and lived almost as far away from the U.P. as his sister. He might have loved me. But he couldn't raise me.

My mother (I subsequently learned) thought Carl was a drunk. They weren't close. She was closer to John, whatever this actually meant. (I spent the summer in Waycross when I was thirteen.) What must the two sons have actually thought either of each other or of their sister? Did John want to get out of Calumet as bad as my mother did? Could Carl have been secretly pleased (hence that smile) to see them go—and now me?

Finally, what of me? What did I think as I stood on the runway and tried to conceal my feelings? Certainly I must have been still shocked at Granny's death and all the fearful, unknown consequences it immediately had for me. More deeply still, though, did I feel more like an orphan, who had suddenly lost his mother (and no matter that he was now being claimed by his biological mother)? Or did I feel akin to a foster child, who had been already without a mother, and was now about to get another home (and no matter that this new one was that of his biological mother)? In the picture, you can't tell.

In memory, I retain only one fact: vomiting on the plane. Everybody is anxious for me to settle down. I vomit anyway. Either before or after I do so, I am taken up to the cabin and shown all the instruments by the captain. Does this calm me? I don't remember. To where did this single-engine Wisconsin Central plane fly anyway? Detroit? Chicago? Could I in fact have vomited on the second leg of the flight to Los Angeles? I don't think so. By then, Calumet would have felt too utterly left behind.

Back to the two photographs: what moves me about them now is how emotionally saturated by Calumet each is. The attire of both my mother and me is a bit too flashy for the somber mood. Even the weather conspires; the sky is overcast—snow is very likely on the way. (It must be late fall.) The arms of Carl's two kids—or, as I seem fitfully to remember, his wife's kids—are swinging side-to-side, as if they're cold in their sweatshirts, and want to get home.

One detail especially strikes me. In the first picture, Carl has a small suitcase in one hand and a bundle in the other. The suitcase is surely my mother's; I remember its snap locks. The bundle looks like it contains food for the trip, put in some sort of plastic container and wrapped in a cloth. Maybe his wife made pasties!

How touching to see that in 1952 air travel—granted, this flight was a short run—still retained the intimate character of an automobile trip or a train trip. People who saw you off made sure you had something to eat later. Carl's wife was doing her best. Perhaps, as a mother, she had a more tolerant, and then sympathetic, feeling about me than her husband did. I don't think he made the pasties (let's call them).

In any case, other than my own mother, who doesn't look quite ready for the role, Carl's wife is the only thing this photo has going for it, maternally. I want to believe not only that she made the pasties but that she made them with something resembling Granny's love. So let's say that after the plane took off, and then attained maximum altitude and cruising speed, I opened the bundle and ate one of the pasties. Too bad it was too late for pasties. Too bad I vomited.

Hal

Was my father notified that Granny had died? Did he think of attending the funeral? Was he somehow part of the conversation that agreed I should now pass to my mother? Most likely, the answer to all these questions—none of which I ever asked him—is, no. He would say this was because he was never allowed contact with me. Everybody else would say, either that he never wanted any or that he and *his* family were simply too threatening to my welfare.

Growing up in Calumet, I knew I had a father. I never knew he had a family. Forty years later, during the first time I revisited Calumet, my wife found out that in fact my father's family lived just down the street from the home of my grandparents! How is it possible I never knew this? Once my mother told me that she, Granny, and everybody else were afraid my father's family would "steal" me. Over time, I gathered, this became an article of faith. It never had to be tested.

Did I write to my father? Surely, yes—and surely he wrote to me, since his business, when I got to know him, was advertising. Memory fails me again, though. He made one visit, or one visit I remember, at Christmas. The only thing that's lasting in my mind—other than everybody assuring me, "this is your father"—is that this big man sat on the metal chair I had just been given, and bent the legs so bad it was unusable. Talk about symbolism! Maybe everybody else was right: this man and all he represented (whatever it was) was just too threatening.

Therefore, again the rightness of Tobola solution: the complete absence of Caesars from my life. If I said I didn't miss my father, it might sound either untrue or cold or both. But I don't believe I missed him. I was aware he existed, somewhere south of the U.P. One day I supposed I would see him. Meanwhile, new snow was falling, there was another comic to read or a movie to see, Granny was making pasties again tonight, Gramps might take me for a walk tomorrow afternoon, and where were we kids going to meet to smoke next week?

In fact, I next saw my father when I was fifteen. My mother brought him to my boarding school and the two of us met in the lobby of a nearby hotel. I was confused, not to say baffled. Why had this man—this father—arrived now? He said, a special trip; my mother said, a business trip. He assured me that he loved me; my mother assured me that he didn't (or else why not give her some money to raise me?). He invited me to live with him in Chicago that next summer; my mother didn't want me to go.

I didn't. Mostly in order to please her, although the decisive reasons may have actually been so immediate— my own friends, things to do—as to be used up in the living. I remember a picture my father gave me of Shelley, his stepdaughter. She was about my age and she was beautiful. How could I not desire to spend time with her? To date, I'd never had a girlfriend. Not going to Chicago was like refusing a proposition of some sort. But what sort? I was still only fifteen.

When I was twenty-nine, I found Harold Caesar's name in a Chicago phone book and wrote to him, proposing that we meet, since I was driving to Chicago anyway. (This was in fact true.) He replied, with directions to his house. I subsequently got lost and at one point found myself in a black area of Chicago. "Maybe I'm going to be more surprised than I expected," I mused. My father liked this line, which broke the ice after I eventually pulled up into his driveway, and he confidently sidled out, mixed drink in hand.

"Call me, Hal," Hal said, "everybody does." Hal had an expansive personality, an affable manner, a fine instinct for what people wanted to hear, especially if it happened to intersect with what he wanted to say. He loved meeting strangers. It took me a while—father and son met periodically over the course of the next ten years—to realize that I was yet another stranger, albeit an especially challenging one, since I happened to be his son. When Hal stole some money from me, under the pretext I was a sort of business partner, we fell out for a few years, and then picked up the relationship for a final ten, until falling out once more, after which Hal died, a few years later.

That first night in Chicago, and on all subsequent nights, especially when we were alone and Hal had been drinking, Hal held forth on two themes: his hatred of Calumet, and his hatred of my mother. Calumet he hated for predictable reasons: too provincial, suffocating, and so on. My mother he hated because she (and my grandparents) had successfully contrived to deny his whole family any contact with me. I couldn't speak to the first of these themes; I loved Calumet, even if my love had never been tested, as his had, by adolescence or young manhood.

Regarding the second theme, I could only nod, resignedly. If somebody tells you about the deprivations of your experience, what exactly to reply, especially if in fact you don't—or didn't—feel these deprivations; in fact, your experience seemed full. I felt sorry not for myself but for Hal. The poor bastard had been born in Calumet, and eventually spent his life getting out and staying out. But what about my broken desk chair? He didn't remember breaking it, he didn't remember the visit.

So at age twenty-nine, for better or worse, I finally had a father. This was precisely at the moment I was about to lose a wife; I was in Chicago to pick up her up, after a visit to her family in Los Angeles, whereupon we would drive back to Pennsylvania and separate. As Hal and I were waiting for her at the train station, I remarked to him it would be hard for me to love him, because he had never raised me—he had never refused to let me drive the car, I had never hated him. Hal didn't like me saying this. So we shared more respective memories of Calumet, and tried to pretend we had each grown up in the same place in the same way.

V

Me in My Stroller

Mother

Once a few years before she died my mother and I were driving. She suddenly blurted out a memory of how hurt she was that once when she visited me in Calumet I refused to fly away with her in order to spend a night in Chicago. "How old was I?" She didn't remember. "Why did you want me to go to Chicago with you?" No answer. "Can you imagine how afraid I might have been to leave?" She couldn't imagine.

So it always went with all my inquiries into my Calumet past. My mother was more disinclined to commit acts of memory than anyone else I have met in my life. Because she was haunted by some deep, pervasive guilt? This sounds too glib. And it ignores the element of aggression either in her responses to questions or in the articulation of her own memories. Finally, guilt slights what I can only characterize as my mother's canniness: she had an answer ready for any line of inquiry, and these answers never deviated.

Hence, for example, why had I been living with my grandparents in the first place? Because she had divorced my father. But why didn't I remain with her? Because she had to work Why did she have to work? On this question, inquiry ceased. Obviously she needed money, obviously work was the only way to get some. Why (I reasoned) even bother mentioning day care or child support?

In fact, why bother to explore anything else about this time? How exactly (and with whom) did I get from Rockford, Illinois—where I was born—to Calumet? After all, Rockford is hundreds of miles away from Calumet, and it must have been a much longer drive in 1942 Who drove? Oh, and by the way, what year was that, exactly? 1943? Idle questions all—dismissed, many of them, so long ago, that neither of us remembered anymore the first time they were posed. But, really, who wants to remember anyway? "It happened so long ago."

Only my mother's resentment remained, and so the only one left from this time that still had juice was the question of what happened in, or to, the marriage? It's always seemed to me whatever it was was pretty sudden—and so the decision to leave me at my grandparents had a hasty, ad hoc character. Therefore, my father's explanation—given once, late at night, after plenty to drink, in a Washington DC hotel room—rings true: he caught my mother in bed with his brother.

My mother was always content either to imply or strongly suggest that the fault lay with instead with her husband's womanizing. He was even fooling around— once she all but stated—on the morning she gave birth to me! This explanation has always seemed to me perfectly consonant with Hal's character. Gradually, though, I came to feel that both explanations had their truth, just as divergent explanations did in my own divorce. So why bother pursuing the fatuity of some definitive truth?

A formula sufficed my mother nicely about a final matter: what my grandparents actually felt about receiving a child, me, into their home. Did they need him? Did they have to be persuaded? (Did mother or father or both offer child support? Was a fixed period of stay agreed upon? Etc.) Over the years my mother said repeatedly concerning the reality of her taking me back: "it would have killed my mother." Of course, given this, she never had to mention when she might first have liked to have had me back, much less explore her own responsibility to consider the consequences on her mother after handing me over.

I can't be sure what Gramps or Granny might have expressed about such mysteries. They must have told me something, communicated some attitude, uttered some resentment or apprehension. Could this be why I lack a final memory during my years in Calumet: a single visit from my mother? There must have been one. Sometimes, I can almost reach it—through a whiff of perfume (my mother loved it), a blotch of color (she loved loud clothes), or the air of some distinguished arrival (as my mother's would have been). But then my grip on the event dissolves. I'm left with nothing substantial.

Impossible, though, to shake some felt connection between her and that toy canon. Could it have been a gift from my mother? (I recall no toy of mine remotely like this one.) If so, how irresistibly psychological to speculate that in repeatedly shooting the damn little canon ball, so annoying to everybody, I was in fact working out some sort of aggression against my mother. Inwardly, I held her responsible for abandoning me and I hated her for it. But if thoughts now of her "guilt" seem glib, so do thoughts about my "hatred."

What seems to me more clear is that I was simply and profoundly afraid of my mother. Two reasons. First, she came loaded with emotional baggage—her own as well as mine. She preferred all her life to keep the lid on. To this day, I can't unpack everything. Second, my mother threatened to take me away from Gramps and Granny. I loved them both. Gramps and Granny wanted me when no one else did. (So I must have reasoned.) They were my real parents, and Calumet was my real home.

The time before I had a mother was the most continuously happy period of my life. I had everything a child could want. (Except unlimited comic books and a little more lime juice.) Of course, my childhood had to end. Every childhood has to end. How ironic, though, that mine ended at the moment I came into possession of a mother, who by this time had come to represent just about everything I did not want, most especially a love that subsequently felt, as feared, too vain, distracted, and rife with perfume.

How sad, too, that the end of my childhood had to mean the loss of Calumet, Michigan. When I saw it again forty years later I almost cried. To walk the streets once more was to feel faint. The town is so small! (Gramps's post office, say, not even two blocks away from home.). Just so, how small a child's world! And yet Calumet—poor, remote Calumet, with its grey skies and its gray people, its abandoned mines and its empty streets—once constituted the entirety of the whole world to me. I couldn't bear the knowledge that to see Calumet again was to see it lost.

About the Author

Terry Caesar was formerly Professor of American literature at Mukogawa University in Japan as well as Professor of English at Clarion University. He is the author or co-editor of eight books, most recently *Speaking of Animals. Essays on Dogs and Others* (Brill, 2009).